The Zieglers and Their Apple Orchard

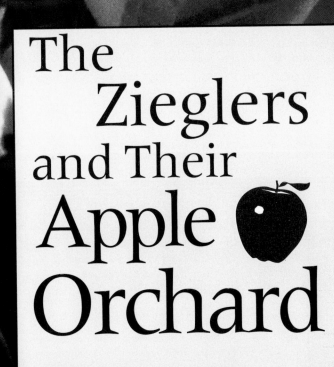

written by
ALICE K. FLANAGAN

photographs by
ROMIE FLANAGAN

Reading Consultant
LINDA CORNWELL
Learning Resource Consultant
Indiana Department of Education

CHILDREN'S PRESS® *A Division of Grolier Publishing*
New York • London • Hong Kong • Sydney • Danbury, Connecticut

Special thanks to the Zieglers
for allowing us to tell their story.

The Zieglers would like to dedicate this book to their children and grandchildren,
especially to those who have not yet been born and may never see this orchard.

Visit Children's Press® on the Internet at:
http://publishing.grolier.com

Author's Note: The Zieglers' last name is pronounced ZEE-gler.

The photo on page 11 was taken by Mr. Ziegler.

Library of Congress Cataloging-in-Publication Data

Flanagan, Alice K.
    The Zieglers and their apple orchard / written by Alice K. Flanagan;
photographs by Romie Flanagan.
        p. cm. — (Our neighborhood)
    Summary: Follows the different kinds of work that the Zieglers do
in their apple orchard beginning with fall pruning and ending with
picking and selling the ripened fruit.
    ISBN 0-516-21134-X (lib.bdg.)   0-516-26471-0 (pbk.)
    1. Apples—Juvenile literature. 2. Apple growers—Juvenile litera-
ture. [1. Apples. 2. Apple growers. 3. Occupations.] I. Flanagan,
Romie, ill. II. Title. III. Series: Our neighborhood (New York, N.Y.)
SB363.F58 1999
634'.11—dc21   98-18917
                                                               CIP
                                                               AC

Photographs ©: Romie Flanagan

Mr. and Mrs. Ziegler own a large apple orchard in Illinois.

They live in the orchard in a beautiful house.

From their house, they can see their
orchard of 1,500 apple trees.

Mr. and Mrs. Ziegler are always very busy. From late fall to spring, they prune, or trim, the trees.

Mr. Ziegler saws the large branches and sells them as firewood.

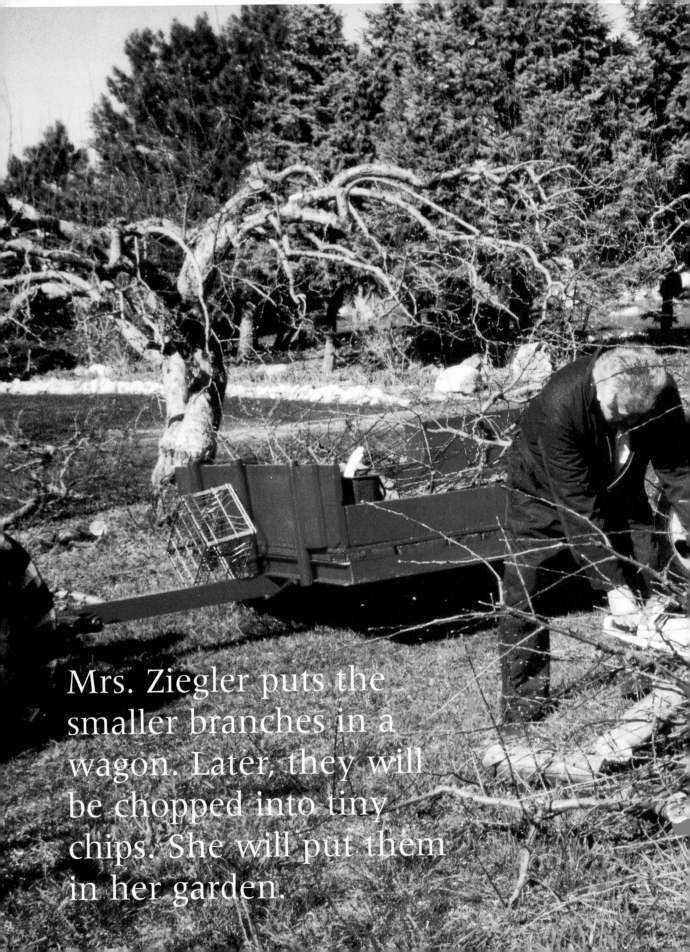

Mrs. Ziegler puts the smaller branches in a wagon. Later, they will be chopped into tiny chips. She will put them in her garden.

9

The trees go through many changes
during the year. Their first leaves
appear in April.

By May, the trees are covered with tiny flowers, called blossoms.

As soon as the trees blossom, the Zieglers bring hives of honeybees to the orchard.

The bees collect sweet nectar and yellow pollen from the blossoms. Then they take both to their hives to make honey.

Bees collect the pollen in special pouches on their back legs.
As the bees visit each flower, they leave behind some of the pollen. This is called pollination.

Apple blossoms need to be pollinated so that the fruit will grow.

Mr. Ziegler sprays the trees with special chemicals to keep them healthy. The chemicals keep harmful insects and fungus away.

Mr. Ziegler also cuts the grass around the trees so hungry mice and rabbits won't nest in the grass and eat the bark of the trees.

Every day, Mrs. Ziegler drives her truck through the orchard to check on the trees.

Some of the early apples are ready to be eaten by the second week of September.

Then the Zieglers open the orchard. Many people come to pick apples and have fun.

Some adults have been coming to the Zieglers' orchard ever since they were children. Now they bring their own children.

Families look forward to picking apples every year. It's a tradition.

Even the Zieglers pick apples.

Sometimes, they get help from one of their sons.

The Zieglers sort and polish the apples. Then they sell the apples in their store.

Every year, the Zieglers make delicious apple juice called sweet cider to sell in their store.

28

And no one goes home without buying one of Mrs. Ziegler's famous homemade apple strudels!

Mr. and Mrs. Ziegler are happy at the end of a good season. Their hard work paid off. The trees gave them a good crop of apples.

Then winter comes, and the orchard freezes. The trees store their energy. They will need it for new growth in the spring.

Meet the Author
and the Photographer

Alice and Romie Flanagan live in Chicago, Illinois, and have been involved in publishing for many years. Alice is a writer, and Romie is a photographer. As husband and wife, they enjoy working together closely. They hope their books help children learn about the people in their community and how their jobs affect the neighborhood.